Sylph

Date: 10/7/14

Abigail Cloud

Sylph

Lena-Miles Wever Todd Poetry Series / Pleiades Press
Warrensburg, Missouri & Rock Hill, South Carolina

Library of Congress Control Number: 2014931676
ISBN: 978-0-8071-5693-3 (pbk.)

Published by Pleiades Press

Department of English
University of Central Missouri
Warrensburg, Missouri 64093

&

Department of English
Winthrop University
Rock Hill, South Carolina 29733

Distributed by Louisiana State University Press

Cover Image: Louise Richardson, "Tatting," detail

Book design by Wayne Miller
Author's photo by Sarah Peterson

2 4 6 8 9 7 5 3 1
First Pleiades Press Printing, 2014

Financial Assistance for this project
has been provided by the Missouri
Arts Council, a state agency.

For Ruth Elliene and Nichol Asher

Contents

The White Act

Apothéose

Acknowledgments

Thank you to the editors of the following magazines, in which these poems first appeared:

American Poetry Review: "The Everyday Demon Experiences Burnout," "Cicada Killer #1," "Cicada Killer #2," "Cicada Killer #3," and "Tryst"
Backwards City Review: "Blue Birth Demon" and "Birth of the Everyday Demon"
Black Warrior Review: "Snapped Key Demon"
The Cincinnati Review: "Earth Star" and "Blind Woman Walking Barefoot in Rain"
Copper Nickel: "Needle Prick Demon" and "Burying"
Cream City Review: "Angel Goes on a Bender" and "Demon of Hidden Birds"
The Gettysburg Review: "After Failure," "The Christening," and "The Girl with the Enamel Eyes"
Gingerbread House: "Choked Peppermint Demon"
The GW Review: "The Ox and the Waterfall" and "The Crib, 1864, Utica Asylum"
Paper Street: "Weaver"
Parnassus Literary Journal: "Ginger at 3 am"
Pleiades: "Bones" and "Lunatic Notes, 1838"
Quarter After Eight: "Swan Aubade"
Quarterly West: "Potato"
Salamander: "Spider"
Southern Humanities Review: "Mad Scene"

Thank you to Wayne Miller and Kathryn Nuernberger at Pleiades Press for their careful attention to *Sylph*, to Dana Levin for choosing it and advising me in its polishing, and to Louise Richardson for her art. Thank you to Mary Ann Samyn and Aimee Nezhukumatathil.

Profound thanks to my family for their love and encouragement, and special thanks to my sister, Sarah Peterson, for reading and commenting on *Sylph* in its early days. Thank you also to Mark Jenkins for his comments, and to Larissa Szporluk, Sharona Muir, John Wylam, and my MFA and *Mid-American Review* colleagues at Bowling Green State University for their early eyes on some of these poems. Thanks to Mary Biddinger for the Winter Wheat workshop that inspired this book, and to Theda Assiff, Mark Taylor, and Dixie Durr for educating the self that dances.

PROLOGUE

White Night Demon

Crickets scramble over the eyes, scratch a gavotte
into the lens. There is no tincture to quiet

these fiddles, no balm to slow the spinning
wheel. Even the silk, so much a vow, falls

in ropes. Nightgowns slither in a box. The valance
chivies at the sash. The legs, all puppetry

sticks, work a fire in the sheets, worry their iced
snap. A faint bare thread sighs loose

in a gash, now a mouth. The feet elaborate
claws in the dampest hours. A dark spot

on the forehead bores back through the fog,
swells time with ifs—a whisper to smooth

the palm. A hiss of white to slice a dream open.
The weight of albati to hush such hard

walls, to vague each new pitch, all the harsh tickings.

The Birth of the Everyday Demon

murmurs to the surface
long before a day is over.
Its pale mother, silent, bone-
dry, squats and dreams her child
released. The lock that holds
the key stuck. The shoe nail
thrumming bruise into the heel.
That other baby born a breathless
shade of blue and a desperate
lull until it squalls. Mother
knows the baby will make damage
stronger than these, and then forgets
it ever existed, leaves it to lie
in a cold puddle. The baby
builds its own hot cave, whispers
its own new name. It chooses
a future like a low-burning headache.

Needle Prick Demon

The bead drained red in a thousand
tiny rivers, bleeding into a slow

muslin wave. The flayed finger
stuck once too deep by the incisor

slicing down and down, the crisp
hands once too dull against

its angles. How the bulb of ache
began spreading into the cold

wrists. How the tongue felt bruised
and stained sucking at the raw

wound. How the crystal had held
warm and whole to the white

stretch for a perfect second before
the weave drank it down and in.

Broken Jar Demon

Stop—a slurry of flashes,
fingers crisp with parsley
and the sudden absence,

a violent gap. How
the synapse connects,
a splinter of fear in the nail-

bed. The light twists,
the car has been in one piece
for five more months, the cat

is still purring at our ankles,
the doorbell never rang.
Curse all these numb

figments. The assembly
of shards cannot be a sign.
The air blisters.

The Demon of Untraceable Scents

You'll do a double take with the air, chin
a sharp compass to a sudden choir
of darts to the nose. Time, its wooden

>   core, will split open. That day, the ground
>   threw them. No, your face fell
>   to meet them, bird's wings, money, a fist

full of peels, just leaves in a pile, his laughter
dangling out of reach. You squirmed
in that burrow, turned to meet October

>   hail, shriveled stars clattering over the grass
>   like egg shells. Your nose itched
>   with a pastiche of allergy and too much

thinking, too much cider, and a splint
of coffee, mouthwash, his fall cologne caught
in your own hair. But he was never so there

>   as he will be when you can't find him
>   at all, stalling madly in that impossible draft.
>   You will be sure that if you turn your head just

one inch, everything will make sense again.
Sidewalk. New smoke. Mums. Blank air
that will pass in a spray of hours to seal the day shut.

Lost Wedding Ring Demon

You remember the miracle of gold letters,
a clip of rings. Some day you will need butter
to slim that finger to undress it before your heart
is opened. Now, the flash pockets into a drain,
slides into the only crack in the pine floor,
drops one, two, black, in the tangle
under the porch. Today it is unlucky,
because it's the 13th, or the day your brother
was born. Or the night you wished
to announce your new dream. If you think
about it long enough, and you can't help
this, you will know it's the opening of a dark
gate. Because isn't that what good demons
do? Bottle your faith into one small object, pressed
like the taut skin of a bubble not yet breathed
forward?

The Christening

Family affairs are ever thus: someone is left
off the list, because there aren't enough dish
domes, "Crystal Fountain" is so close to "Brackish
Pond," and didn't she die eighty years ago

anyway? This malevolent aunt-smoke stalks
into the party, takes a drop too much whisky,
and drizzles invective into your cradle: You
will never be loved, or you will get pregnant

as if in your sleep. *I once knew a girl who closed
her eyes and bore twins. She woke up old.*
The aunt's spindled dogma winds around
you like magic, twists a century of *cauchemar*,

all dragons and thorns. Someone snatches
you up before you believe, dangles lilacs
above your nose, promises princes and cake,
the gift of song, and lips like the red, red rose.

The Girl with Enamel Eyes

Those men like catapults, their cow-white
    eyes, they never saw the trick of it. She slipped
into my corner, put her hands on my breasts.

She skinned her nails into my back—the half-
    moons did not leak or anger. She stole my frock
and turned me over a chair in a heap, tossed

my book to the floor. My father swooned
    over his alchemy. Her Franz's ladder rattled
at my window. I want to tell him we do not all

love him and his fence of teeth. She smiled
    like a clock. She took my place. Her feet traced
all my patterns. The one-man band told me

she will be to him all women. I am not his
instrument. But I have seen him pin a butterfly
to his collar. I have seen their sawdust heads

cracked with beer. They have mocked me
    in my balcony, their arrowed fingers dig out
the air. I'll never see the blessing of the bells,

or dance the hours. But when she bent low
    to the sheaves (He loves me, he loves me not)
I am the one who heard the wheat.

Before the Glass Slipper

Ashes aren't so bad—
Cleaner than dirt, and softer.
White in the center
where the filth is burned
out. *I am good.* Some
shrivel like shells
or cherry blossoms.

At times I'm between white
trees in a snail coach, sliding.
It's strange. I'll curl here,
very close to the fire,
and the cinders will seal
around me until I turn diamond.
Then my skin shines,

cold and latticed and satin.
The charwoman told me
I will stay in the palace
and rest at his feet.
I will wear corsets
and whisper. I will let him
perfect me.

From the Compendium of Old Madge

To warm a woman's feet.

Bathe the feet in a mash of mint
and powdered clove. At night, sprinkle
cayenne and ginger at the foot
of the bed. If married, consider lettuce
to reduce incidental effects, or feed
the husband sunflower seeds to render
him impotent.

To quiet a man's rage.

If a man is chronically enraged, avoid
the nightshade. Rather, drops of violet
in his tea, laced with orange blossom,
will induce sleep. Or, a lady may heighten
a man's prowess, and so combat
his energy—vervain for hair growth,
fruit of eryngium for libido and gum pain.
If the rage be sudden, give a tisane
of star anise and thyme in rum, drunk
all at once, and let him alone until calm.

To view the future.

Crush a scant handful of hazel nuts
and contemplate their shape. Eventide,
take to your bed with a pillow of mugwort.
You will dream of loved ones or learn
to conquer a fear. Take care the mugwort
does not moulder, lest your future also
decay. Burn the pillow for a pleasant
smoke.

To render a person young.

Pass a new quail's egg over the body
to absorb contempt and regret. Explain
to the egg, as it hardens. Bury the egg
in a failed well. Rinse the body with
a wash of elder flower and ash. Extract
a promise against grain liquors and jealousy.

To ward off fright.

Make a tea of tansy, valerian root,
and elecampagne. While the tea
is drunk, sweep the body with cedar
branches tied with basil, then sprinkle
the head with cayenne. If the shock
be off a broken heart, bind the chest
with heartsease and tie the girl
to her bed at night, lest the wilis
tempt her.

To bind a woman to a man.

At dinner, burn an incense of cinnamon
and hang a patch of myrtle above
the table. Or, if the lady's choice
is not desired, feed her a cake
of periwinkle ground with houseleek.
Ignore the mandrake root unless
the lady be a sylph. Do not speak,
lest the spell be upset.

To ground a sprite.

To keep a fairy, you must remove
her wings. In a fire, char the roots

of sea holly and mandrake. Grind
these in a basin. In a kettle, burn
as many moths as are drawn to the fire.
Add to the basin with a scruple
of clematis juice. Drop into this
mixture a length of scraped muslin,
light in the air. When the sylph
comes to you, wrap her in the scarf.
Her wings will shrivel to be plucked
away, or drift to the ground
of their own accord.

THE BLACK ACT

James Pursues

Poor cake. Poor unwedded rings, chirps
in a jar. Let's tell a love story about sleep

and its thread. He lifts her layer straight
from his dream. She blends past his eye,

his eye *en papillote* with the crisp *battu*
of wings. The leaves of his honesty peel

away from the branch, his other woman
a brusque needle dropped in the woods.

From within this *boîte*, he follows the wisp's
trail of snow eryngoes, candied love charms

that melt with her hair. He makes himself
a parable. Her feet can never praise his hearth,

no wax or honey to collect her shade. Enter
the old lady and her cantrips—fists of bees

and scruples of eggs, a promise: One scarf—
how like tissue—one kiss. Her wings

will snap to the dust, tsk tsk tsk. All the evers
ever imaginable. She will stay on his ground.

Siegfried is full of improbable vows

Siegfried sharpens his arrows nightly.
Siegfried has been (accurately) accused of stuffing.
Siegfried and the boys are out for a hunt.

Siegfried thinks red against white is erotic, like a poinsettia in the snow,
    or blood on a feather.
Siegfried finds he's attracted to swans.
Siegfried thinks a swan is like a woman.

Siegfried thinks this swan is a woman.
Siegfried has never seen such a sharp line of birds, as if they are tied
    to a stake or a spotlight.
Siegfried would throw himself in front of a gun.

Siegfried wonders if a swan might be too much trouble.
Siegfried wonders if black is really a more attractive color.
Siegfried is shedding masses of diamonds, silks beyond price, and
    maybe his wits.

Siegfried sees lamplight on a throat as a warning.
Siegfried wants to fight someone immediately.
Siegfried will never go to the woods again.

Siegfried is in the woods again.
Siegfried tries his best to grow wings.
Siegfried would throw himself into her lake.

Cicada Killer #2: Soldier

The week the mail stopped,
the cicada killers defended
their territory. They fought
their wars. We discussed
boundaries and how a woman
may shift the wasps' homeland
with a few dowel rods, a few blond
borders; how the males will fall

in line and keep to new rules.
We know it's best if they are cowed
by our giant wishes. We talked
about the nature of wings
and how, to test trespassers,
the males simply try to mate
with everything.

Earth Star

Ten slick eyes
aghast from all the black
seeing, clinging to the bark.

She was never awake
to him, just moss
sponging at her back.

She felt the eyes,
saw one tight pop,
a flesh of spores

diffusing. The itch
of them breathing
over her arm.

Tryst

The whirlybird moon, the spangles
in the cloud of her skirt, a leopard
pump hide-and-seeking in a curl
of the blankets. Her nerves banged
an anthem to the sexy Bartlett
pears, the sexy palm plant draped
in the corner, the mirror like a mouth
on the wall. She made her excuses
to the nosy cherubs on the lamps,
muffled their commentary with scarves.
She knew there would be mock
goodnights, a fractional vocabulary.
She knew a belt would get looped
around the bedpost, a candle snuffed
out with a thumb pad. The sexy china
bull. The sexy coat rack. The cherubs
knew it would all end in smoke.

In Which Angel Goes on a Bender

Angel binged all night in the hayloft, a rabid
mush of poker and schnapps, the cards
slipping over burnt skin, her long

nose reddened. A pack of charred cards,
an old woman crumbled into the dust. Black frost
on the hayloft rim, a ruined edge.

Her old pack of cards, a bottle
of something hot. Burning snaps slip
over the cards, a rabid old woman

in the hay. Skin reddened at the rim of the loft,
a pack of cards slipping over the edge. Frost
on the tip of her nose, a hot poker long in the woman

spread out in the hay, a bottle of something spilling
over the night.

Bonnie Parker, After the Second Heist

(My mother always said) Patience is a virtue,
(revenge is a dish) best served cold,
(gathering slow freeze) in a meat locker.
(Bank on it:) My debutante palace waits—
(Change is in) the wind,
(our sapphire future) building like jackals in the sky.
(They call us) Barbarians—I just want
(a new pair of shoes,) to sit still,
(together in spring;) I can guarantee
(your gold, my silver,) my sentiment, iridium
(in our crucible) my love. We are like lightning
(in Texas—) too fast for every town.
(We're in too deep) For prayer.
(Lamb, these yellow words) Under our black rhythms
(are boats to richness,) are forests of treason.
(Our fires) Whet my appetite
(for ambition) with need; rebellions
(are a tide) that shepherd us to death.

Ginger, at 3 a.m.

Our bedroom is always immaculate.
I am the type of girl
who can wear a satin and marabou
gown to bed and wake up
with it on the next morning.
You might be wondering if he
wears that tux to bed,
and I hope it won't disappoint
you that he doesn't.
Instead, he wears white pajamas.
We both wear white.
Everything is white.
Dancing is the only thing
we still do at night.
Sometimes I wear red
and we don't even do that.

Ginger's Stylist Tells All

I hate it when she comes in at nine
in the morning and can't open
her eyes wide enough to curl
her lashes. They stick together
with a black Don't-ask-me
kind of sludge, and I don't ask,
but she murmurs: "I wonder

what it would be like if I woke
up and my legs wouldn't work
and no one knew why. It happened
to a woman I knew; she loved
to dance." Those are the mornings
she asks for a bucket of cold water
for her feet. "If it happens, I leave

my pointy shoes to you." Fred
comes in as bright as new snow
and she stares right through him.
"I don't know what to do with
my skirts. Taffeta is too big
for wheelchairs, and no one
but doctors will look anymore."

But what I want to say is this:
What kind of girl goes to bed
with her makeup on?

Nights at the Moulin

The habit of pain and smiling
after shows. Nails ache from her fingers,
her wrists keen to the bar. The fat one—

keeping his drink out of her lap.
She tells him the story: "I was once
a bird of fire and they wanted

the feathers of my body. There is still
fire behind my teeth." She is tired
of not being alone.

She rested in her cottons
then. Now there are knees
and thunder, broken heels, the fluff

and fall of color, rips, the others
in the line: "But weren't we fantastic
ogres tonight?" If she never had to leave

the lights, she'd be happy. Thoughts
sit on her thighs and she wishes
just once she could dance with a cello,

to assume its gravity, legs kept round
and low underneath. Here, they are after her,
her shoulders white like the inside

scrape of water, stage lips too siren,
the face on her waist. These are all paper
men. There is no body—

Remember this. The fat one. The painter.
The dreamer in black wanting it
with one hand.

Spider

She asks you to solve her riddle
and you can't get around all the legs

posed in her parlor, her form contorted
and enormous, toes picking arbitrary

ornaments into the silk. This mannerist,
always female, always a legend,

is lying in wait to suck them dry,
all the good bees in her parlor. Decipher

her existential question and she will eat
her mysterious smile. You can bind

her web over your most damaged
places. "Can sleepers desert

their bodies?" You must answer
before she releases you to her tunnels

the question, still black in her parlor.

Mattress Fire Demon

But the splash of water
did not squash the red eyes
entirely. Sometime in the night

the world below the heavy
body melts, a thin crust
between the clammy skin

and hell. How like home
for those hot little hands,
those black teeth like knives.

They twist into the cloud-
soft dreams, weave their tattery
garments whole. The end is a shriek

of acrid laughter, their clawed
mouths working through the hair,
sucking at the scorched cries.

Snapped Key Demon

You knew it the second
the brass scraped into the lock,
teeth bucking the groove
and the involuntary twist
of the wrist a new disaster.
A sharp clap and the heart
comes away in your hand.

How can the day have ended
so broken, your fingers curled
hot over bits of a hundred
people's lives, their eyes locked
with yours for so many half-
seconds? You've absorbed far
too much of their worry

today, worked over all
their mute grief. Your own
longing is tattered in their
accidental fists, the other half
wrenched immobile in the bolt.
How much it's taken from you.
How unmoved this door.

The Everyday Demon Experiences Burn-Out

Something on the water. Something
wholesome, like spoiling corn crops
or sparking a tri-state wildfire. Or
a bit of glamour, like stopping glass
elevators in casinos, between floors,

then dropping them. I'm tired
of small catastrophe, the delicate
balance between shrugged-off accident
and tiny horror. Fits of pique, bursts
of desperate memory, tireless, dull

annoyance: How many brittle ankles
can be wrenched in holes? How many
jugs of milk can be soured before time?
How many smashed heirlooms, rained-
out parades, singed fingertips, coins

dropped in grates, stained blouses
before business meetings? How
many shiny balloons are there still
to burst?

The Demon of Unlucky Strikes

The trick is to be convinced
he doesn't care about you
at all. Will your limbs
to be rubber, the very worst
conductor, your knees already
aquiver in their sockets. Fear
is its own lightning rod.
Guess how many streetlamps
he would rather have. Walk soft,
heels toes. Don't let him hear
your legs snapping. Forgive
your mother. Refuse to be
galvanized. Think, "I won't
be the highest point." Duck.
Remember everything you know
about ice. When you come
to trees, be one of them, not worth
any effort. Think pure thoughts.
High heels may buy you time—
he seeks out more challenging
targets first. Wear clean
underwear. Forget everything
you've ever learned about
electrons. Forget you've never
been in love. When you can't stand
it any longer, run. Believe
he won't even trouble to look.

Outside the Glass Factory, Murano

Maybe I'm too narrative
when I say his observation
of my naked thigh was almost
hot enough. This man knows
what pain is, how it might be wanting
quiet, but also unwrapping wounds
in the sun. I want him to forget
my thigh, the siren knee;
I'm no figurine blown in tens
and sold for 10,000 lire or dinner
on the mainland. No, we won't
be *incalmo*, two shapes fused.
I know he would touch my leg
if he dared, but we are both
made of glass, a cracked girl, a boy
too malleable, and he will melt
if he stays in this heat.

Cimitero di San Michele, Diaghilev's Grave

But I went and loved the old man. I touched his stone. I imagined the ground quivering underneath. I know he never laughed, but his feet were busy and I loved him. I coveted the two beaten birds on top of his grave, but they weren't the birds, just a pair of shoes. The feet weren't inside anymore, but maybe they were, cut loose from a girl, to shake in the wind. I would cut my feet off for him. I would give him all my blood.

Dancer's Poem for Callas

I dream your voice into my body,
your sound thin fibers in the text
of me. We are spoons
stirred from outside ourselves,
your coloratura, my red shoes.

I have seen you half-lost,
hair black against the film and hands
twined at your neck, fingers curled
to your cheek. This touch—grief,
the folds of your dress sharp with it.

You once refused to sing.
When you stood still your audience
writhed, breathed   *La Divina*
in their seats, transmuting the language
of your hands, your chin. Your eyes
honest like your life is not one
long secret.

Maria, you chose the wrong art.
How many now let you shiver
into them, tell them what to fear?
What if   then   the ache
of your mute throat for the first time

I cannot speak.
The pain of your silence   *follie*
would have driven them mad.

Postcards for My Mother, Galleria Borghese

Proserpina

I am afraid to eat pomegranates,
to gnash their seeds,
small red eyes.
Their juice is smoke
that swallows me
so you would never find me.

Hands can press my flesh,
pull me through the earth;
but Mother, I will not be queen.

Dafne

I would run like she did
but I could never be a tree,
feet dead to summer.
My fingers are never
still and my hair has always
loved the wind.

Mother, I would run
but I would not scream.
I would let him catch me.

David

There is a storm, armies
outside the windows
and I am frozen mid-step,

my words half-heard.
We are balanced, ready
to release it all to the air.

I am always between.
Mother, I can't kill all
the giants.

La Verità

The truth is unfinished.

Mad Scene

In this poem Giselle will whisper
in Albrecht's ear. "My love
is too big; it splits my spine
like snappish wings. I know

you will betray me. I see
her corsets in your waking eye."
In moments she'll be mad,
chase a moth through the laces

of her cincher, tangle herself
in her mother's hair, and scratch
a thumbnail down her own cheek.
She will hold air in her hands

like a bird, like her heart, like his
heart, like a sword. No tree
grows high enough to fall
from. No skirts could drink

enough of a river. Her feet
will grow too wild for shoes,
her mouth too desperate for words.
Her hunger will drive her through

the wood. In this poem it will
not matter that no red stains
spread over her waist. It will
not matter that shades close

in like severe owls alighting.
It will not matter that he is guilty.

THE WHITE ACT

Myrtha's Woods

One cold spear of wind can peel a man's
skin from his chest. We empty his heart.

We forget his name. I spike their fury
with wings before they can remember

love. We've each tumbled
out of that dirt. I am never unhappy.

Wili

The trees melt in the village. Night, its breath,
shades the leaves into silence. Her feet pluck
impatience under the earth. All the bones

in the square are hers. Her hand plucks
thistles, bends them into wings. Leaves
cast poems over her arms. In her eye

the village melts, its thatch and sugar
glass. The roots grow in filigree through
the bones of her cottage. Her feet bend

into wings. The trees square off with thistles,
their leaves hinging into the night. Moths,
like glass, silence his torch. Scarves

of shade melt out of the village. His fever
moths the night with searching, its roots
plucking at her bones. Her wings cast poems

over the glass of the earth. His eye bends
through the bristling trees. When the light
sugars the leaves, her shade melts out of his hand.

The Ptarmigan

It's soft as ritual
scratching the ground.
Mornings, the tight smell
of dust, the flicker of feeding.
Count the perfect eggs. Check
and check.

Cold, it goes back to the grounds,
clean north. Flock north.

Trace these scratchings
over white white white.
Do it or the danger—foxes.
The nest is not round. It places
the twigs. The owl will stay
out. Place them again.

Cicada Killer #3: Matriarch

Did you see her, at rest on the porch
rail? Twin humps, or a lion clutching
a zebra. How horrible to be a mother

long before you're a mother, the bulge
of the ichored veins, heave and heft
of nourishing an egg, laid to pulse

in subconscious pits, the sand tickled
out like feathers. How delicious
this cicada once was when this wasp

was a baby, when all these wasps
were babies, their white eyes blinking
out at their mothermade dark.

After Failure

Between the broken cradle and her chest, her breath.
A vow. A curl of cotton. Wings impaired by sleep—
its absence. This is not the last nuit blanche, the last

white bird without ascension, listening for safe
dreams. How could dreams or words make any difference?
This silk. This falcon, this one diamond. Feathers. Rocks.

A cloud. She smashes all the things worth splintering,
remembers all the oracles' wan lies, clean robes,
their ashen faces. How they told her, "Rest." Her hair

goes slack. Her mouth works curses for them all and then
forgets. She waits for visitation with its flock
of hope. She marks her vigilance with stones. She counts

her sins like spies, like arrows. Where's the lamp against
this snowstorm? Resurrection up from this blind cave?
A lily drops its petals in a halo. Skins

on shapeless apples age and darken. Silver spoons
in drawers arrange to rattle. Everything might gasp
an answer, turn the air, its clotted hush, to cream.

Water at the Lunatic Ball

The room was full of water.
They floated everywhere.
     The one who forgot her husband's name.
     The one who thought his feet bled.
     The one who didn't want her skin.
All their faces—garish in the gaslights,
their forms damp and heaped
inside their borrowed gowns and jackets.
You, hot and shapeless in your muslin.
You wanted to drink but you knew
their slow, calming poisons. So you danced
with the one who tied ribbons on his ankles,
as the band flew loose from time,
a floating waltz tangled
in your legs and chest, your neck
stretched high. He had you then
and it was okay to drift and tell
the truth, your secret stories.
To feel the suck and shrush
of the wet and to let all their hands
touch you and pull you in.

Library

You are lost when you sleep,
which is why, when you find it
underground, there is no system
to correlate death, psychology,
bird, glass, nerve. And the pages
fall there, unsheaving, unbinding
the air. So that glass hurts when
it dies. Schizophrenia smelts grit
into quail. Egrets bend under
stress and hide in the ground.
And what about all the assertion?
No fact is solid. The point
of the dream is not that there is
no map, but that nerve and bird
are the same lesson.

Bones

What is bone? Bread in your body. A core—the ground. Words that speak all the time of a yellowing of dream, its truth rusting to black and splintering. It's sharp and you can't remember why. Guilt gutters in the center, shrieking outward in points. What is guilt? A time when other minds rush inside your own, as many as slip past your gates.

Lunatic Notes, 1838

Case: A young girl who paid no attention
to anything. She felt the hot iron (they say
a torrent of fire strikes their frames) and promised
reason. Maniacs rarely fail in this respect.

Case: A man said he was quite black,
but had no corporeal disease and slept
without derangement. After a year
of horse exercise I told him he was a disgrace
and successfully combated the disease.

Case: The old woman refused to know
her husband. When he visited, she met him
with pleasant vagueness. Treatment with cold
lotion to the head had no effect; however, she is
a favorite of the staff and no trouble to anyone.

Case: He claims to have received a divine command
not to eat. We find the tube in the nostrils preferable
to knocking out the front teeth. Patient finds
he can be made to live.

The Crib, 1864, Utica Asylum

A patient who slept in the Utica crib for several days commented that he had rested better and found it useful for "all crazy fellows as I, whose spirit is willing, but whose flesh is weak." (Journal of Insanity, October 1864.) University of Iowa Hospitals and Clinics Medical Museum

Sister, you asked where they put me
when my mind crawled away
from my body. Lie flat in a bush.
Let it catch you, your weight pressed
out between tight fingers. There are eight
points—the tips of your blades, the bulbs
of your hips, the knob of your tailbone, the thud
of your heels, the bell of your skull. Balance
on them. You will feel pain until it is numb
and the bones bulge through the flesh.
The sky falls to your nose and waits
for you to grow sane.

Letter to a Suicidal Man

Leaving is falling away.
You do it backwards and forget
to turn around and look.
I've already wept at the weary
methods in squirrel hoards
this autumn and the lull
of speech in the store.

Once there was a man who went
into a mine and he was heavy
and stayed there. They say
his wife packed him a lunch
and he left it on the kitchen table
and that's where she found it
before they told her.

I look through the window and see
you sitting on the edge of the bed.
I know it will have something
to do with water. I will let you
go, the way the light sweats
through the glass and sinks
down the curtains this morning.

To a husband and son lost in fog

You are in a hollow, a sand-
beaten cave. His poor, white
feet lick out at the sieve,
the shiver of slipping
away. The break of tide
with silence. Tell our son
he is asleep wadded up
in his blankets. His heels
are held down to earth. Tell
him, Child, your wings
have a while to grow. The fog
is only the scrim of my skin,
my hair peppered crisp against
your chest. I cannot stop this.
I sent you out in a perfect
sweater, a clutch against chill,
but even I, I who already taste
the rind of your drowning,
cannot unwrap it. The new flood
creases under your feet, fills
the menace of pools, the living sand.

Choked Peppermint Demon

Pillow sucked snug
to the face. Wind
force-blown down
the throat. Ton
of water clapped
tight to the lungs:
I had my choice
of time and place.
They call us gasp
demons. Last
week my brother
killed a thousand
fish. His agent—
a bear wedged
over the stream
hole. So much
oxygen stopped.
My father stuffed
socks into vacuum
hoses. Mother
squeezed swimmers
breathless. But
I need sudden
panic of air,
cold drop of a day
passed quick
into fear. Eyes
that roll. Fists
and tears. I wait
in parking lots
of pizzerias most,
look for wrappers
tossed to the ground.
Then, it's easy—

a poke, or slap,
maybe no more
than a hiss.
That sweet white
disk, the potent
stripes, slips fast
down the pipe,
stuck tight over
shrieks. Desperate
gulps the lung
can't swallow.
I know too well
how soon a sleeve's
caught, the pulse,
the ricochet
and shatter.

Blue Birth Demon

Fascia of blue bells explode
in the eye, a well-thumbed
petal, veins broken loose

through a tiny rip. My blue husband
is here; Angel, he is angry
and has no idea what kind

of smoke covers us. What
kind of blue you were. Never
in my life could I hear

such a blue sound, such a dark
cream to the ear. Cold
is a principle only blue

children understand. All this time
a shell crackled empty
in a nest, a milk jar rattled

beside the door. A sad slip
of paper curdles.

The Demon of Hidden Birds

One sawing on a misplaced
branch, its feathers only
imaginable. I'm telling you:
It was not a bird, the air
too unreasonable, the branches
nude. Did I mention
it was screeching into
silence like it had no hope
of rescue? No, it's a trap—
its sound like that of my only
child. Tell me the baby
is not high in a dark cradle.
Tell me these shavings
are not his sky dropping.

Swan Aubade

At dawn the feathers shriek
through our pores like smoke.
Our bones shrink from their marrow,

the seams of our clavicles
steamed flat.

No nettle shirt and star
flowers, no six-year silence
to molt our wings permanently
to wrists.

Ours is an uncommon spell.

Your arrow should have struck
me through, my plumes plucked
for the hat of your bride. You will wake
from me in that forest, our flotilla
a crenellated dream.

At dawn I am numbered
by the Swan Master. At dusk,
by God.

Pray for dogs to break
the circle. Pray for poison
in the sedge.

My neck is always half
your heart.

APOTHÉOSE

Bayadère

Their tongues fashioned baskets
of asps. They turned their backs
to pantomime and commanded

my unwinding devotions, my legs
uneven candles arched to Indra.
My limbs haunt one thousand

sleeps, their married dance.
In the kingdom, I ravel the edge
of the veil. My breast waits

for our taut space to reconcile.
I pray to the north. I pray
to the bare sky. At the end,

the temple will collapse to smoke,
uprooted pavilions in that thin place.

Husbandry

Remember the hollow, the ill-stained
skirt. Remember the discreet mutter
of wrens. They warned you to keep
leagues away from his wood.

> His price your mantle?
> His price your ring?

You hoped not. (Of course, you snugged
your garters up tight, well over your knee.)
One plucked rose, once to the well. At home,
green mornings birth nothing but questions.

> Father's in pieces.
> Mother's in church.

Your story: He swore himself a mortal,
snatched by the fey for ransom to hell.
Why not believe? Much nicer than tatting,
listening to courtiers grouse in their beards.

> *I'll not name the smith.*
> *I'll not name the squire.*

To Miles Cross then, at mirk and midnight
(who could ignore instructions like these?).
Look for the white horse, a cocked-up
hat (he said), and haul that rider down.

> Adder, bear, eel, esk,
> grayhound, lion, scorching spear.

Dip him in milk. Your thefted prize—
a naked man. Dip him in water. Cover
him (or don't), and wrest him clear
of sparking rye—the fey queen's on fire.

　　　She'd pluck out his heart.
　　　She'd poke out your eyes.

Ignore this. Now, remember the babe,
your father, your naked man's freedom
(all yours). Remember his pants, hie
away to the church (Girl, marry him, do).

　　　Your price his ring.

Shades

Night moths so fast in the waking trees.
Slow wings devour echoes. Wait

a short time. Echoes. Nervure stretched
in the garden, our bodies chime

in the trees. We collect silver, fast over
the ground, our price speech,

our forgetting breath. Our nerves tear
our bodies and make them no

bodies. The garden's thoughts braid
into pinions. Moth echoes devour

seeds of speech. At dawn, the light pliés
to the west. The thrushes take

enchaîné to the sky. Our breath slips
over their hollow wings, silver

devotions of time. Hot trees enchant
our nervure. In the night's

changement, we collect chimes and speech,
set the ground to waking, and fall,

our simple dawn, to earth.

Cicada Killer #1

First
there is the wrestling
from reverse graves
of dirt. Reticulate
wings spear into July.
No spells. No cauldrons
of birth. One new body
pacing the firehot
walls, naming each old
thing again and again,
a revision of earth. I am.
I am. I hear the humming
all the way out of the garden.

The Ox and the Waterfall

To remember you bob your head in
and out of the fall of the shower.
This is what breathing is like

for oxen, nodding always
like nothing will ever surprise
them. They keep to the ground,

furrowed as their brow folds,
but maybe oxen have waterfalls
too, rivers that push to abandon

their channels. They wait ten years
to be sure no one is looking, then
slip over the edge and run.

Some of the water gets tired
and settles a lake, but some rushes
headlong toward cliffs to forget.

They do it for the air. There is also
freedom. Let it go and go with it.
Learn to stand where the water wants

to be. It will ask you to move.
You will have a choice. If you want
to, fall, or throw it all down to begin with.

Blind Woman Walks Barefoot in Rain

under the scissoring sky.
Its dingy laundry breaks loose
from the line, cuts down
to earth, claps over her feet.
She is mother to everywhere,
out of touch with these pinching
salts. Her hands curl
around the known: a cane,
a pair of shoes. Her bare
toes squelch into the empty
mud, into the scrim of chatter
filling the distance.
My agony for her is a rock,
a worm—pink and bruised—
lost under the heel, a thousand
tiny shards of glass. But her feet
bless equal measures of raindrops,
fevered, asking—in summer,
how can you say no to the ground?

Potato

Understand this: green is the color
most difficult to light.
It hides until it is more painful
to burrow than to belong.
Love may or may not be like this.
Then it stands square to the earth,
browns in the air—skin and faith
come to wrinkle and believe.
And why not famine? Because cheap
life is more durable and warm.
Green hovers overhead and knows
that knowing is like fur and hot
and water. When there isn't moon
the center glows inside out,
sheds its wrappings in a heap,
white moons bare as day.
And green shrinks back, fades, tries
to furrow in the red dirt.

Thanksgiving

The cranes circle the blue
house, its neighborhood,

its small town. I have a stone
of grace in my throat. A story

of grain. A starry great night
spread on the lake. *khu-rruk*

A man and a woman call
hymns to the other's vessel,

store up ephahs of breath
in each cup. Snow chaps

the air. They fold their
streams of wind into wings.

Sylphide

In somewhere nests there are owls, flumes
of moon in the dark. On the lake, four swans
in the snow. In the looking glass, I loved
you. In the blink the mouse spent
to disappear, I loved you. I cannot stand

the sight of rings. By the lintel, our lady's
candlestick. Beyond the hedgerows, sea
holly. The tansy will not forget. I had
to touch your sleeping eyes, capture all
their vows. I loved you from the mantelpiece.

I loved you in the chest of drawers. I loved
you while the creeping mallows stretched
and ebbed. Out on the ice, a silent cave.
I could not wait for your eyes to open. Today,
the lavender rotted in its patch. The thunder

cracked this tree. I cannot build my wings
with clay, I cannot build my wings with lace.
I loved you hidden under the tartan, behind
the curtain, just past the pane. I loved you sifted
into your lamplight. I loved you nestled

on the highest shelf. Under the cat's fur. Between
the door and not door. The buckthorn kills
all my enchantments like weeds. I loved you
pressed against the glass. I have great sympathy
for moths. Have I gotten what I deserved?

Burying

When it rains this way
you're happy.
So slow you can find a drop
and follow it into the ground.
There's the order
of it, the closure of sound,
because isn't that what you worried
about when he was gone? In that false
quiet there was no speaking,
just the need. You were raised
not to scream and that's all
you did, words behind your teeth
and your tongue straining.
Now you let the rain do it
for you, but slowly for a while
so you can count what is said.

About the Author

Originally from Bath, Michigan, ABIGAIL CLOUD has published poems in *American Poetry Review, Black Warrior Review, The Cincinnati Review, Copper Nickel, The Gettysburg Review, Pleiades, Quarterly West, Southern Humanities Review,* and elsewhere. She is on the faculty at Bowling Green State University, where she serves as Editor-in-Chief of *Mid-American Review.*

About the Series

The editors and directors of the Lena-Miles Wever Todd Poetry Series select 10-15 finalists from among those submitted each year. A judge of national renown then chooses one winner for publication. All selections are made blind to authorship in an open competition for which any North American poet is eligible. Lena-Miles Wever Todd Prize-winning books are distributed by Louisiana State University Press.

Previous Winners

The Glacier's Wake, by Katy Didden
(selected by Melissa Kwasny)

Paradise, Indiana by Bruce Snider
(selected by Alice Friman)

What's This, Bombardier? by Ryan Flaherty
(selected by Alan Michael Parker)

Self-Portrait with Expletives by Kevin Clark
(selected by Martha Collins)

Pacific Shooter by Susan Parr
(selected by Susan Mitchell)

It was a terrible cloud at twilight by Alessandra Lynch
(selected by James Richardson)

Compulsions of Silkworms & Bees by Julianna Baggott
(selected by Linda Bierds)

Snow House by Brian Swann
(selected by John Koethe)

Motherhouse by Kathleen Jesme
(selected by Thylias Moss)

Lure by Nils Michals
(selected by Judy Jordan)

The Green Girls by John Blair
(selected by Cornelius Eady)

A Sacrificial Zinc by Matthew Cooperman
(selected by Susan Ludvigson)

The Light in Our Houses by Al Maginnes
(selected by Betty Adcock)

Strange Wood by Kevin Prufer
(selected by Andrea Hollander Budy)